En Otro Oz

poems by

Chantel Acevedo

Finishing Line Press
Georgetown, Kentucky

En Otro Oz

ACKNOWLEDGMENTS

I am grateful to the following literary magazines for their support of these
poems, which appear in the chapbook:

"Leaving la Habana, that Other Oz." *Cimarron Review.* "Dorotéa Remembers
Oz, Seen from the Inside of a Hot Air Balloon." *Cimarron Review.* "Brujas."
Diode Poetry Journal. "Avian Exile." *Diode Poetry Journal.* "Rubies in Her Ears."
Valparaiso Review. "Dorotéa Considers the Scarecrow's Offer," "Rusted, or the
Tin Man's Lament," and "A Metallic Offering" *Saw Palm: Florida Literature and
Art*

My gratitude to early readers of these poems, including authors Ash Parsons,
Dorraine Bennett, and poet Keetje Kuipers. Your support and feedback have
been invaluable.

Thanks to Aaron Alford for his beautiful cover design, Carrie Weir for her
friendship and photography skills, and author Margarita Engle, for her support
of Latina writers everywhere.

Editor: Christen Kincaid
Cover Art: Carrie Weir
Author Photo: Orlando Acevedo
Cover Design: Aaron Alford

Printed in the USA on acid-free paper.
Order online: www.finishinglinepress.com
             also available on amazon.com

Author inquiries and mail orders:
Finishing Line Press
P. O. Box 1626
Georgetown, Kentucky 40324
U. S. A.

Table of Contents

Rubies in Her Ears 1

Tía Em's Prayer 2

Dorotéa's Inheritance 3

Brujas 4

A Catechism in Oz 5

A Lighted Match 7

Doroféa Considers the Scarecrow's Offer 8

The Inconvenience of Flesh 9

Rusted, or the Tin Man's Lament 10

A Metallic Offering 11

They Now Came Upon More and More of the Big

    Scarlet Poppies 13

Why the Lion Wasn't Interested 15

The Guardian at the Gate 16

The Wizard Seduces Doroféa 17

Avian Exile 18

En Otro Oz 20

There's No Place 22

Doroféa Remembers the Sea and Havana from the Inside

    of a Hot Air Balloon 23

To poet Emma Bolden, who first encouraged me to write poetry in the first place. All of the couches, Em.

Now we can cross the *Shifting Sands*.
—Frank L. Baum's last words to his wife, Maud

I dream with my eyes
Open, and day
And night I always dream
—José Martí, Cuban poet and patriot

Rubies in Her Ears

Four weeks old, the needle, rum-dipped,
      held fast between the pads of her
      father's fingers—
her mother could not keep her hands
      still enough, palsied by her animal
      need to shield—
his paw heavy on her tiny forehead, fingers
      so long they spanned her whole face—
      hand filling the universe, hand holding
the needle, threaded with red string, also rum-
      soaked. Thin aguja, thin as a fish bone,
      thrust through the baby's
delicate earlobe, piercing a tender morsel of flesh.
      She cried. Twice for each jab—twice more
      when the thread was pulled through days
later—the abscinded flesh ready for the next
      violation—a pair of rubies—little pinprick
      gems, such brilliant wounds.

Tía Em's Prayer

After her niece boarded the airplane,
Tía Em prayed to *los santos*,
and to Changó, god of thunder,
that her niece be spared turbulence,
airsickness, the winds of a *ciclón*. A slap of lightning
sounds like rifle shot, like the *revolución*.
Tía Em remembers Oz. She's been there,
too, tornado-struck long ago.

How the Emerald City teemed with blood
thirst, its faceted towers limned in red.
Televised executions de rigeur, no more strolls
down golden brick roads.

How like a *ciclón* those ruby days, swirling,
as if a great plug had been pulled, leaving
behind the dross of our dreaming.

Ay Dios mío, protect Dorotéa,
sky-bound, spinning now above me.
May she know nothing of gunfire,
of witchcraft. May she remember home
in her exile.

Dorotéa's Inheritance

After death she dried up quick
in the sun, toes curling up like
fall leaves. The empty slippers had

mouths, tongues lolling
in Oz dirt, licking emerald
dust and ashes. She touched

them, and a panorama of home
fluttered in the atmosphere
before Dorotéa. A clot of low-

slung houses against a gray sky
flickered, then was snuffed
out. A luscious woman in white kissed

Dorotéa's forehead for protection. Still,
the girl could not resist—she crossed
herself, Padre, Hijo e Espiritu Santo,

praying against possessions, mal
de ojo, fungal infections, or whatever
evil the dead bruja had left behind.

Brujas

Oz mothers warn their children
about gathering pennies
or seashells. The island's brujas
cast spells on such things, trapping
their green-skinned miseries in those
copper disks, in the grooves
of Apple Blossom shells, which are painted
pink like the dawn and are so hard
to pass up. Oz mothers say, "Rattle a sand dollar
and what do you hear? The shimmy of a dozen
ills and heartbreaks, mal de ojo, curses.
Keep away from such small beauties."

Oz mothers pass the brujas by on their way
to work. They cross themselves, make
rough t's on their childrens' foreheads, mutter
curses of their own: *May a house fall on you.*

Mainly, the brujas smoke cigars
like men. Tourists snap pictures of them,
colorful as they are. For a few Euros
tossed into a reed basket they puff. They grow sick.
Yet through the spicy tobacco haze, the brujas
can see their mothers, grandmothers, great
greats and all the way down the line,
across the Atlantic to that other coast,
where Yoruban chanters taught the first
brujas to capture sadness in ragged
whispers, stowing agony in the kinds of small
vessels that little hands love to touch.

A Catechism in Oz

We sit in rows, six by
six. Red scarves bloom
about our necks. Somos pioneros,
pioneers like el Ché. We will
be like Ché. In all ways, like Ché.

Maestra says fold
your hands in prayer
and ask God for candy.
Our heads hang low
in anticipation of His

honeyed mysteries.
But when we open our eyes,
our desks are bare, save
for some scribbling—*Glenda loves
Tik Tok 4-eva.*

Maestra says pray
to Oz. I feel a flick of life at my
fingertips. Did you feel it,too?
When we look, there, at last,
are green lollipops,

false as seaglass.
Teacher says Oz keeps hearts
in all shapes and sizes on a shelf.
In his head are brains enough
for all of us. Courage he keeps

in a gold-lidded pot that threatens
to boil over every so often.
Oz, our Dios Santo, our Great
and our Terrible, provides. See
the proof of it, slick in our mouths.

How does your sucker
taste? Isn't it sweet?

A Lighted Match

A cold night, another *apagón*—
The lights go dead in Havana as if smothered
by giant fingertips.

Mercury sinks, voices grow cottony,
soft. Overhead, clinquant stars.
The Straw Man lends a tuft of hay

from his forearm for kindling.
The embers shimmer—suns trapped
in the hay. *¿Más?* Dorotéa asks.

Toma, the Straw Man says,
offering a bundle of rosemary from behind his ears.
Brainless, yet he knows the hunger fire

feels for straw, the human apetite for burning—
a pica of the skin that craves heat's
searing breath, it's orange flavor, bright as a Miami sunset.

His painted-on mouth registers the pain of it, of his inner self
going up in smoke. *Un poquito, nada mas*, Dorotéa begs and begs
until nothing is left of the Straw Man but his tempera face.

Dorotéa Considers the Scarecrow's Offer

He said he'd call forth the birds, el tocororo first, of course, that
patriotic songbird. He claimed he could line up peacocks for

me, that they'd march out of the zoo, purling their feathers into
a jewel-toned bed for us. A thousand seagulls could be

counted on to darken the sky, a clot of them lengthening the
night. For us, jackdaws, churlish and sleek, would guard the

atmosphere against winged primates. The birds do not fear him.
Rather, they taught him slumberous songs, the architecture of

nests, the feel of a cricket's tiny pulse thrumming inside a wet
gullet, the sound of a hatchling's hungry shriek. How to fly is the

next lesson. Scarecrow is working on it, crow-taught, though
they peck at this ears and so diminish him. He can teach me how

to leave Oz for good, on currents of air. In return, I might curl
myself like a fern against him. Scarecrow's chest is a bale of hay,

a pillow for my head. Tonight, he made a dandelion chain,
braided it into my hair with fingers that crackled like dry palms.

His hands are cowhide gloves. They scratched my cheeks and scalp,
fumbled my blue ribbons. "Think on it," he said as he wove plait to

stem, ever the logician. "Take me with you, Dorotéa. Trade my rough
touch for the freedom of flight."

The Inconvenience of Flesh

Once, before they met the Lion,
Dorotéa tripped, fell tumbling down

A knoll, tearing her knees, the palms
Of both hands, her chin.

Tin Man fainted upon seeing the first
Crimson drops, and had to be brought

To by the dog, who licked his cheek
With a dry tongue.

Scarecrow observed Dorotéa minister
To her wounds. He, who had watched

As the farmer stuffed his arms and torso
With straw, and who, even now, feared no

Mortal harm save a lit match,
Stood in wonder as the girl sucked the blood

On her left knee, crying softly for her Tía Em,
Who would have come quick with ice and a song—

Sana, sana, colita de rana.
Struck by its inconvenience,

And seeing winged shapes in the darkening sky,
Scarecrow second-guessed his desire for gray

Matter, for opening himself up to the
Terrible possibilities of blood.

Rusted, or The Tin Man's Lament

I've been groaning for more than a year, rusted into stillness
        by salt breezes. Boys play baseball nearby, with avocado
tree branches for bats. Balls thwack my cheeks, thump against
        hollow thighs. I groan. They play. In summer, sirens sound
warnings of cyclones on the way. Windows are boarded shut. I
        remain, mute, wet, stuck. Once, I saw a house fall out of the
sky. In winter, pigeons roost in my empty chest. Their coos set my
        teeth tingling. I like to imagine their tiny hearts thrumming.
Once, a man pried open my mouth, reached down my throat, and
        plucked a gray bird from me. For fun, he dashed the little
thing on the ground at my feet. Afflicted with emptiness and stillness,
        heartless by design, I can do nothing save witness the
bleaching of diminutive bones.

A Metallic Offering

You and I
might join neatly—
you, prim, gingham-checked.
Me, a contraption of fat
joints and clanging parts:

my belly, un tambór, for you
to drum a rumba out of me.
I have a pennywhistle, too, for you to play.
I know you have a song
inside, notes arcing from your mouth like rainbows.

Sing to me about the place
you come from, the house
the Gales own, the land that belongs
to them, to you, and no one else.
Promise that you'll make room

for me—in alcove, in cellar,
in the casing of a grandfather clock.
I will tick melodiously for you.
I promise to make myself profitable.
Take my collarbone, I'll fashion

a diadem of tin for you, mi princesa
americana. Shave my skin. Gather
the dust of me in your cupped hands.
See how it looks like crushed diamonds?
Smuggle me out of Oz, my silver-footed

girl. I'll make room for you in my
commodious chest, if you'll make room
for me on your gray-scaled farm. Give
me three rows of cornfield, an oilcan,
a place to call mine.

**They Now Came Upon More and More of the Big Scarlet
Poppies.**

I

Focused on the serious business of trying
to get out of Oz, Dorotéa didn't consider

the many ways a plot twists, thwarting desire:

There could be snakes lying in the clusters of flowers.
There could be vines, ready to trip a girl, snap an ankle.
There could be sleep. There could be starvation.

Cloying fumes like twisters up the nose
send Dorotéa sprawling, along with the dog
and the lion. Felled like a tree, for a moment
she wonders if the Tin Man chopped her down.

The flowers shift, hiss at one another—*tendril, petal.*
Gloom sets in. Dorotéa dreams she has reached the sea, her silver
shoes are sucked off her feet by the lapping water. Her toes
are white worms. She breathes a wish—I want off of Oz.

II

Meanwhile, Tin Man and Scarecrow decide which
of the sleepers they will save. Lion is too heavy.
The dog fits inside Tin Man's hollow chest. Easy enough.
The girl lies in Tin Man's arms. Scarecrow is too weak

to carry anything, his muscles composed of
dry grass, sprigs of rosemary. He has a corn cob spine.
A shame to lose Lion, they think. A coward, yes, but
the big ones are useful. One mighty bite from his jaws

And enemies are vanquished. Scarecrow imagines the
great creature starving in his sleep, his carcass food for crows
that so plagued Scarecrow in his salad days. An easy
choice—girl over lion. Draped in his arms, she makes

Tin Man feel manly. Had he a heart, it would be filled with
heroic pride. Dorotéa nuzzles his cold chest, presses
her lips against the rivets holding Tin Man together.
She dreams of schooners, dinghies, rubber rafts.

Other possibilities do not disturb her sleep:

There could be tourists, wind-swept from dry, flat places
or snowy, barren ones, who long to touch an ochre ringlet
in exchange for coins, for nothing, for a taste of a free man's skin.
The poppies draw them in droves. Such bright Caribbean colors.

Why Lion Wasn't Interested

The flare in her throat where her pulse flickered
palely was, obviously, a draw.

Her blood thrumming there so warm, so warm. Imagine
my felted paws on her cheeks, twitching, tightening.

Hombres, her eyes are glossy like aggies, darting
a mile-long view down the road of yellow brick.

What cat can resist such sudden movement?

But she called me a baby, *señores*, swiped my snout
with a cold, flat hand. Her calloused fingers a shock, a shaming.

What man can permit such a thing?

Dorotéa doesn't know that Oz men have a pulse that beats
like bongo drums, barks *Babalú ayé*, Ricky Ricardo style.

We know how to spank a misbehaving woman. Ay, Dorotéa!
She gazed at me like a colonel. Like a tiny dictator.

Stormy-eyed witch, I want no part of her. She brings me to tears.
Shameful tears! I'll bet she tastes like Eden fruit.

I'll take one bitter bite, that is all, and spit her out. Let the Wizard
take her back. I'll spot her in the sky and feel myself grow brave.

The Guardian at the Gate, a Triolet

If you come to Oz, we will give you green glasses,
emerald glasses, they can't be removed.
Green for the lads! Green for the lasses!
If you come to Oz, we will give you green glasses.
Put down your basket! Your oilcan! Your axes!
A green world like ours will numb you, will soothe
if you come to Oz. We will give you green glasses.
Emerald glasses. They can't be removed.

The Wizard Seduces Dorotéa

Come my sweet poppet, my ombre-
eyed darling, to sit before me, Indian-
style, like the Taínos, who, roasted
on spits long-ago, taught the seductive
language of Oz—*roads, witches, houses, gravity*—
then were silenced. I will tell you the way a man
bounces on airstreams, communes with flocks
of parrotlets, those downy smudges of green. See
me, child, dangling beneath a technicolored
balloon. Whoosh. Vaporous heat.
Volatile flight. I imagine I am an emerald dragon.
I dream of setting fire to miniscule cities, and men
of straw, watch them light, hear the shuffle of kindling
feet scratching the earth, dancing while they burn.
Upon landing, I dub myself great and terrible.
I don't need to ask who you are, or why you seek me.
I have a story for you, poppet.
One you need like air.

Avian Exile

1

The spill of men's hearts, poppy red,
had been televised, and she had watched
the way she once watched tropical lightning
—astonished and awed by its ripping violence.

She once cupped her hands around the sun,
holding its rays like yarn between her fingers
casting on those burning beams, the new world
long and furled out in her vision.

2

Her lips, metallic from too much kissing,
formed familiar words, no longer fresh words.
So many crushed campaigns, so many others spat
off the island. Dearest plovers, dry beaked people

with little wet wings. They descended somewhere north,
woke in that place knowing their last day
would dawn under a strange firmament,
their eulogies spoken in foreign mouths.

3

Now, men on green thrones trade hot contention
for black SAABS and ancient rhetoric.
She gets it now, in the last second, heavy,
hanging between death, dead.

Drowned in a bucket of water.
She takes rain and rusts out, reduced to minerals.
Her skull turns to glass. Winged things pluck at her
As her tongue curls into curses.

En Otro Oz

Dorotéa wraps her lips around the Tin Man's
party favor nose. His blue marble eyes
cross while she plays him like a salsa flute.
His belly, a hollow barrel, catches
her breath that swirls in that dark
space, seeking heartstrings to pluck.

The appalling vibrations exit through his
Fingertips. It is the sound a conch shell makes
when blown, sending the Taínos out to war,
or else, a warning blast upon sighting
three puffed sails—Nina, Pinta, Santa María.
The waves slow their lapping. The sea is

dazed by the sound and takes on the look
of flattened tin. The Tin Man trembles at
the sight. But Dorotéa, her voice sweet and
silky as coconut milk, calms the metal man:
"A smooth sea makes for better swimming.
Who needs a wizard or a hot air balloon?"

Flat on her back, Dorotéa's shoulder blades
furrow the water. Tin Man thumps his chest, yells
"I can't swim!" There is the clang of his metal
feet, like water smacking a buoy. His belly
rumbles. Now, the current pulls a song out
from him. He rolls in the surf. He is a tossed can.

Dorotéa cries out for a witch wearing yellow
and blue, the colors of la Virgencita,
and of Yemayá, Mary's African double.
Maybe she will float down, cradling a small boy,
or else carry driftwood and dry seaweed to
kindle a ritual fire and dry out the sea

There's No Place

A witch once tried to teach Dorotéa about
      connotations. *Home. House.* Brainy,
whole-hearted, the girl had no *home/house,*
      not since it was smashed. The place
where you hang your silver slippers lacks
      a lexicon, she thinks. One whiff of Tía Em's
kitchen—musty rice smells in the main—
      and syntax fails. The sighing sounds of neighbors
sinking into one another at night results in a tongue
      knit by pleasure. What is home? A house?
Tornado-whipped, a house starts to pitch, is orphaned
      on a roadside, a flood of yellow in the foyer,
its front porch falling down. Uncertain, Dorotéa
      repeats after the witch, her heels kissing,
clicking, asserting what she wished she knew for sure.

Dorotéa Remembers the Sea and Havana from the Inside of a Hot Air Balloon

Tía, I will tell you what I saw
from the inside of a hot air balloon basket
headed north to Miami. The jagged Malecón,
the seawall holding Oz in,
glowed green in the moonlight.

Ay, colór esmeralda, Dorotéa's tía says.

Yes! And the sea rose up every thirty seconds
to greet the wall in a rush of foam and spray. In
the street, vendors set up wares—trinkets carved of
teak and the hairy shells of coconuts. In the sea,
dark shadows of sharks spun lazily.

Sí, m'ija, Dorotéa's tía says, there are sharks
in the waters of Oz. Tía rolls up her skirt. There
is a silver scar on her thigh shaped like a moon,
the size of a small bull shark's mouth.

When the wizard pulled me closer to the basket's rim
I resisted, kicking his shins. What if I felt the urge to jump
in? Who would catch me below? The Tin Man couldn't
swim. Scarecrow would probably write a poem about it,
about the day I disappeared over the sea.

Tía, it would be a beautiful poem.
Perhaps he would turn me into an ink mermaid,
or pencil me into the lighthouse beams on the bluffs of Oz.
I could have jumped. Been a slender shadow in the gloaming,
a beam over the water, a beacon for those leaving Oz.

If only it were true, says Tía. Por Diós.

Chantel Acevedo's novels include *Love and Ghost Letters* (St. Martin's Press), which won the Latino International Book Award and was a finalist for the Connecticut Book of the Year, *Song of the Red Cloak*, a historical novel for young adults, *A Falling Star* (Carolina Wren Press), winner of the Doris Bakwin Award, and National Bronze Medal IPPY Award, and *The Distant Marvels*, (Europa Editions).

Her fiction and poetry have been nominated for the Pushcart Prize and have appeared in *Prairie Schooner, American Poetry Review, North American Review,* and *Chattahoochee Review,* among others.

Acevedo is currently an Associate Professor of English in the MFA Program of the University of Miami.

www.ingramcontent.com/pod-product-compliance
Lightning Source LLC
LaVergne TN
LVHW091235080426
835509LV00009B/1298